COOL in SCHOOL

Michael-Anne Johns

SCHOLAST
New York Toronto London
Mexico City New Delh

Many thanks to the way cool Randi Reisfeld, Craig Walker, Maria Barbo, Sarah Longacre, Scott Appel, and Sue Schneider.

ISBN 0-439-18848-2

12 11 10 9 8 7 6 5 4 3 2 1 0 1 2 3 4 5/0

Printed in the U.S.A.
First Scholastic Trade printing, July 2000

Front cover: (top left): Lisa Rose/Globe; (middle left): Walter Weissman/Globe; (lower left): Andrea Renault/Globe; (center): Bernhard Kuhmstedt/Retna; (top right): Jeffrey Mayer/Star File; (middle right): Lisa Rose/Globe; (lower right): Mark Allan/Globe. Pages 4-6 (all photos): Seth Poppel Yearbook Archives; Page 7: Bernhard Kuhmstedt/Retna; Page 8 (top right): Globe Photos, Inc.; (bottom left): Seth Poppel Yearbook Archives; Page 9 (all photos): Seth Poppel Yearbook Archives; Page 10: Edie Baskin/Outline; Page 11 (all photos): Seth Poppel Yearbook Archives; Page 12: Everett Collection; Page 13 (all photos): Seth Poppel Yearbook Archives; Page 14: Wilberto Boogaard/Retna; Page 16: Steve Granitz/Retna; Page 17 (left): Gary Marshall/Shooting Star; (right): Larry Busacca/Retna; Page 18 (left): Paul Fenton/Shooting Star; (right): Marion Curtis/DMI; Page 19 (left): Steve Sands/Outline; (right): Mirek Towski/DMI; Page 20 (left): Chaumette/APRF/Shooting Star; (right): Seth Poppel Yearbook Archives; Page 21 (left): Jeff Slocumb/Outline; (right): Courtesy of Scholastic; Page 22: Thomas Lau/Outline; Page 23 (left): Gary Lewis/Retna; (right): Miranda Shen/Celebrity; Page 24 (left): Laura D. Luongo/Shooting Star; (right): Everett Collection; Page 25 (left): Walter Weismann/Globe; (right): David Allocca/DMI; Page 26 (left): Yoram Kahana/Shooting Star; (right): Gary Marshall/Shooting Star; Page 27: John Gladwin/All Action; Page 28: Ron Davis/Shooting Star; Page 29 (left): Courtesy of Animorphs Productions Inc.; (right): Nat Bocking/Shooting Star; Page 30: Steve Granitz/Retna; Page 31: Theo Kingma/Shooting Star; Page 32 (both): Barry King/Shooting Star; Page 33: Paul Fenton/Shooting Star; Page 34: Seth Poppel Yearbook Archives; Page 36: Barry King/Shooting Star; Page 37: Seth Poppel Yearbook Archives; Page 38: Jeff Slocumb/Outline; Page 39: Seth Poppel Yearbook Archives; Page 40 (left): Walter McBride/Retna; (right): Seth Poppel Yearbook Archives; Page 41 (left): Marion Curtis/DMI; (center and right): Seth Poppel Yearbook Archives; Page 42 (left): Bernhard Kuhmstedt/Retna; (center): Courtesy of Animorphs Productions Inc.; (right): Seth Poppel Yearbook Archives; Page 44: Courtesy of LFO; Pages 45-49 (all): Seth Poppel Yearbook Archives.

GUIDE TO WHO'S INSIDE

Introduction

Okay, so the guy next to you in English class isn't Nick Carter or Justin Timberlake, but most of your favorite celebrities did sit in a regular classroom at one time or another. They raised their hands to answer a question, walked up single file to go to freshman orientation, and maybe even got a detention every now and then.

When their showbiz careers took off, many had to switch to a tutor or home-schooling, but it's a good bet they'll never forget those days of hall passes and pop quizzes! On the following pages superstars share their school days' memories — some happy, some poignant, some miserable, and some triumphant. Chances are you can identify.

Guess Who!

Speaking of identifying . . . do you recognize the hotties and honeys in these candid school photos? Check p.35 to see if you're right!

A

B

C

D

E

F

G

H

'N Sync's School Daze

Today, Lance, JC, Justin, Chris, and Joey blend their voices in perfect harmony and kick it onstage with steps to die for. You might say they are totally 'N Sync. However, time travel back a few years, and the guys will admit they didn't always have those smooth moves — in fact, their school days definitely had some "out of sync" moments. Here are their memories.

Schools:

Joey Fatone Jr.: Dr. Phillips High School, Orlando, FL
Lance Bass: Clinton High School, Clinton, MI
JC Chasez: Home-schooled
Justin Timberlake: Home-schooled
Chris Kirkpatrick: Valencia Junior College (he got an associates of arts degree) and Rollins College (he left before he graduated to start 'N Sync)

Joey: "If I could relive any moment in my life, it would be my senior year in high school. I had the most fun and everybody, the whole senior class, was all together and tight. It was just the best experience I had. Seeing everyone when they were freshmen and thinking back on all the things you did when you go to that final day at graduation, it's just the biggest sigh of relief."

Joey: Senior year 1995

Lance: Senior year 1996

Lance: "When I was in school, I used to get in so much trouble every day — just stupid stuff. . . . I sometimes got detention, but not for being bad. I got detention for being late, because I'm late to everything. . . . I also did crazy things to get a girl's attention. I broke into my crush's locker at school and rigged it so that when she opened it up, mistletoe sprang out, and I was standing nearby ready to kiss her."

JC: "I went through a small phase in high school when I was girl crazy."

Justin: Justin's school years were interrupted when he was in the *Mickey Mouse Club* — but after it was cancelled, he felt out of place: "I got so bored and really down about everything. I started getting a little rebellious. I didn't really get into trouble, but I wasn't focusing like I could. I didn't have the inspiration that music gave me, and it hit me: That's my place in the world. That's where I belong."

Mr. Popular!

"I tried to be friends with everybody. One night, I'd go out with this clique, next night, I'd go out with another." — Lance Bass

Brainiac!

In middle school Justin was a straight-A student. When he got his first B, he couldn't believe it! "I was so disappointed," he admits.

Buffy the Vampire Slayer and Angel — Our Wonder Years

The *Buffy* and *Angel* gang have completely different school histories, but whether they went to a public school, a private academy, or a showbiz professional school, they all have vivid memories of those very important years. Read on!

Schools:

Sarah Michelle Gellar: Columbia Grammar and Prep School; Professional Children's School, New York, NY
David Boreanaz: Malvern Prep, Philadelphia, PA
Charisma Carpenter: Chula Vista High School, Chula Vista, CA
Seth Green: Overbrook Park High School, Overbrook Park, PA
Alyson Hannigan: North Hollywood High School, North Hollywood, CA
Nicholas Brendon: Chatsworth High School, Los Angeles, CA

Sarah Michelle Gellar

Sarah: "Elementary school was very difficult for me. On weekends I had to decide whether to go out with all the kids or go to auditions. . . . The second you start missing school, you stop getting invited to parties and people stop talking to you," Sarah also remembers back in 1990. "I had more absences in the first month than you're supposed to have in an entire year. I was telling them I had back problems and had to go to doctors all the time. Then [they saw where I really was] when the TV miniseries *A Woman Named Jackie* aired. . . . It got better when I went to a professional high school and there were other teen actors there."

David Boreanaz

David: "When I was in high school, I was a dork. All I did was play football and stay in my room. The high school years are a trying period of life." David continues: "You know, you have all these hormones racing inside of you. You don't know where you're going. You're stepping left when you should be stepping right. Things are growing on you that you haven't seen growing there before. It's embarrassing. It's frightening."

Charisma Carpenter

Charisma: "I wanted to be a teacher before I was an actress. My friends from high school would never have guessed that. I wasn't a bad student, but I was very social. I had a lot of things going on."

Seth: "For a long time, I tried to fit in with the people at my school. It took me a while to realize that I wasn't like them. I liked to dress differently and listen to other kinds of music. I think people thought I was obnoxious, and I probably was a bit arrogant. Looking back, I'm not proud of that at all, but it was very liberating when I decided that it wasn't important what people thought of me. When I realized that, I became proud of the person I was, instead of trying to cater to other people's perceptions of me. I was a lot happier and could finally focus on the things that mattered to me, like acting and school."

Alyson Hannigan

Alyson: "How did I handle going-back-to-school blues? Not think about it! Or, do you know what's really fun? Going back-to-school shopping. Then it's like, you can create your look."

Nicholas Brendon

Nicholas: "My haven during those dreaded [high school] years was the baseball diamond. As a starting player on the nation's top-ranked high school team in 1988, my junior year, I was dead serious about playing for the Los Angeles Dodgers. But I had to abandon that dream when I hurt my arm a year or so after graduation. Instead, I started thinking about acting."

Backstreet Boys Go to the Head of the Class

The Orlando cuties showed off their talents — and imaginations — even when they were just schoolboys. Have a giggle or two as they remember way back when. Their memories are by turns mischievous, poignant, happy — and musical.

Schools:

Nick Carter: Adams Junior High School, Tampa, FL; then tutored
Brian Littrell: Tates Creek High School, Lexington, KY
Howie Dorough: Edgewater High School, Orlando, FL
A.J. McLean: Osceola High School, Kissimmee, FL
Kevin Richardson: Estill County High School, Irvine, KY

Nick: "One time I was in a school play and I fancied this girl, but she fancied another guy. So I put loads of salt water into the drink that he had to sip in the play. He spat it out onstage!"

Brian: A self-admitted straight-and-narrow kinda guy, Brian says that his early brush with illness — a near-fatal blood infection when he was five — made him look for the positive things in life. "That experience made [me have a] closer relationship with my family, with all my friends, with church, and God. Growing up with that in mind, I stuck to my guns when peer pressure came around in middle school to do what everybody's doing. Instead of going out and partying. . . . I'm not saying I was the best kid in the world, because everybody has flaws. But it just made me a better person."

Howie: "For four years, in elementary school, I was heavily involved in plays, one play after the next. I was a little ham! I would sing higher notes than the girls next to me! I sang in the children's choir at my church, and then I went into the men's choir. I sang throughout high school."

A.J.: "I was a bit of a nerd in school amd was always a little bit different from the others. All of the other kids had a knapsack for their school books and a lunchbox. I had to be different, so I had a briefcase for my books and kept my lunch in a paper bag. For some crazy reason I saw myself as a little business man. For a while I wore glasses, even though my eyesight was perfect, because I thought that they looked cool. I guess I have always been a bit wacky."

Kevin: "I had a great childhood. I loved school, played Pop Warner football, rode horses and dirt bikes, and sang into a hairbrush in front of my bedroom mirror. I got my first keyboard when I was a freshman in high school, and pretty soon I was playing at parties and weddings."

A.J.: Freshman year 1993

Kevin: Senior year 1989

Brian: Junior year 1993

Howie: Junior year 1990

The Name Game!
Under Kevin Richardson's senior yearbook picture is the name Kevin Scott.

Dawson's Creek — Class Notes

Just as they do on TV, the *Creek* kids faced a lot of challenging issues during their real-life school days. Some were tough, others trivial — and some were totally traumatic. See if you can relate to any of them.

Schools:

James Van Der Beek: Cheshire Academy, Cheshire, CT
Michelle Williams: Sante Fe Christian Upper School, San Diego, CA (home-schooled 10th–12th grade)
Katie Holmes: Notre Dame Academy, Toledo, OH
Joshua Jackson: Kitsilano High School, Vancouver (Josh left school his junior year and eventually earned his G.E.D.)

James: Crediting excellent and caring teachers with helping him overcome dyslexia, James says, "They caught it while I was in kindergarten. [I learned to read] in a special experimental class. I didn't even know I was dyslexic until I was [a] junior in high school."

Michelle: "I was actually really unhappy in high school. I got picked on quite a lot. Once, these girls told me a boy I liked really liked me and wanted to meet me at break, so I went, but he wasn't there — it was all a joke. I always felt like an outsider at school. I had occasional friends, but no one close, so I just learned how to be comfortable with my own company."

James: Junior year 1994

Katie : Senior year 1997

Katie: "I went to an all-girl Catholic high school. Every day we'd have to kneel on the floor to be sure that our skirt hems were [no more than] two inches above our knees. I didn't have it super short, but if you had it too long, you were such a dork. You looked like a freshman."

Joshua: Always a cutup, Joshua loved making his fellow students laugh. Says Josh: "I used to get into so much trouble. Cracking jokes and talking when I wasn't supposed to. I would get teachers so mad, they would tell me, 'Just get out of the class!' . . . At fifteen, I didn't take things seriously, and I got kicked out of high school twice — once for attitude and once for lack of attendance. I'd like to say that it was because I was working as an actor a lot, but really, I was just a pain in the butt." Though Josh did earn his G.E.D., he now says he wishes he had studied a bit more while in school. "If I did more work, I probably would have done a little better."

Revenge of the Nerd!

"Who really fits in middle school and high school? I was never, like, the popular kid. That's why I laugh, because *Dawson's Creek* has all these female fans, and I was, like a dork in high school and nobody had a crush on me!" James Van Der Beek

FIVE: Teachers' Pets — Bad Boys!

The lad band called FIVE have a reputation for being fun, frolicsome, forever mischievous. Guess what? That's no act. The British boys were exactly the same way back in school.

Schools:

Scott Robinson: Sylvia Young Stage School of Drama, Essex, England
Abs Breen: Italia Conti Stage School, London

Scott: "I'd been at the Sylvia Young Stage School of Drama for a while when this kid called Renarto Clementa joined. All the teachers told him to stay away from me, but he became my best friend instead! We had a real laugh, but soon we started getting into a lot of trouble. In the end, things got so bad that he ended up being expelled — and he'd only been there a week! I felt really responsible and guilty. . . . I'm not sure why I wasn't expelled."

Ritchie: "I got in trouble at sixth form for going down to [my mom's] pub at lunchtime with my friend because he was upset about failing his driving test. I got what our school called an internal suspension, which meant I had no break times. My mum was all right because she understood that my friend was upset."

J: "I was considered a bad boy in school because I had a mind of my own. I always saw myself as being on the same level as the teachers. So if they said anything which was stupid, I'd tell them. . . . At school teachers used to say, 'Knuckle down now and it'll serve you well.' But I always knew I'd end up doing something like this. I didn't have the best grades. I was intelligent enough to do better, but I didn't do that well because I preferred to entertain people." J was also bothered by those people who took advantage of others. "One thing I couldn't stand in school was bullies. I detest people who bully. It's a sad and pathetic thing to do. If anything, I got into trouble for trying to stop people bullying."

Abs: "I got told off for throwing a bottle at this boy's head once but it wasn't me! My mum came down to the school and it made things worse as the teacher started telling her that I didn't do my homework. I was quite good at school, though."

Sean: "I was picked on a few times at secondary school, but it wasn't for any particular reason. Since then I've learned to walk away from situations like that. . . . [But] in PE, I always used to run at the back, but once I thought, 'Right, I'm a good runner, I'm gonna beat everyone,' so I did. But the teacher said I was mucking about and she swore at me, so I threatened to throw a tennis ball at her head! I got sent home and suspended!"

Britney Spears: Singin' the Mean Ol' Teacher Blues

Seventeen-year-old Britney Spears made music history when her debut CD and her first single, both named ". . . Baby One More Time," entered *Billboard's* album and single charts in tandem as number 1! Wonder if that impressed her first-grade teacher, who seemed to think Miss Spears was a real chatterbox?

School:

Park Lane School, McComb, MS; now being tutored

"When I was in the first grade, I was mortified because I had the meanest teacher. In the first grade, I was the sweetest student, but I talked when she told me not to. But that was because somebody asked me a question and I answered it. The teacher put me on detention! Is that not mean? I had to sit on the steps for recess and I cried the whole time. Mean old teacher!"

Our Favorite Stars Remember

Your favorite stars remember their favorite teachers—and some teachers remember them! They all had favorite classes, too. Are you a science buff? Love history? See which celebrities share your favorite subjects.

Brian Littrell (Backstreet Boys): Brian's choir teacher at Tates Creek High School, Barry Turner, encouraged him to try for a singing career. "I never really pictured myself a singer before that," admits Brian. As an expression of thanks, Brian recently went back home to Lexington, Kentucky, and used Mr. Turner's student choir as backup singers on the song "Perfect Fan" on the Backstreet Boys new album, *Millennium*. Cool!

Jay-Z (rap star): "My parents separated when I was twelve. As for school, I wasn't really interested, but not because I wasn't smart. When I was in the sixth grade [around the time my parents split], I took a reading test and scored on the twelfth-grade level. But I didn't have it in me to work hard. . . . But then I met someone who helped turn my life around—my eighth-grade English teacher, Renee Rosenblum-Lowden. She took our class to her house in Brooklyn on a field trip. You know many teachers who'd take a bunch of black kids to their house?"

Jay-Z

Brian Littrell

Ben Savage (*Boy Meets World*): "The first day of my junior year in high school, I walked into Ms. Pam Davis's American lit class. For the next two years I was in love with English. Previously I had English teachers who concentrated only on structure in our papers—you have to have a thesis statement and three body paragraphs and subsections. But Ms. Davis said, 'Write down what you're thinking, write what you feel, and try to make it come together. I promise, you'll enjoy it.' It clicked and I wrote my first essay on [the poet Ralph Waldo] Emerson and got an A—I didn't have a thesis, I didn't have structure, but Ms. Davis said I had written something amazing. So, for the next two years, not only did I fall in love with Ms. Davis, but I couldn't stop reading. I loved English—I had so much fun in her class. I even wrote my college essay about her."

Andrew Keegan (*10 Things I Hate About You*): "My best teacher was the one who told me to strive for the best—never be satisfied with average grades if you can go for the A's."

Will Friedle

Ben Savage

Adam Sandler

Larisa Oleynik

Will Friedle (*Boy Meets World*): "Mr. Jerry LaChance—he was my English teacher in high school. He didn't treat us like 'underlings'—he treated us with respect, and gave us the liberty and freedom to grow. He prepared us for life."

Larisa Oleynik (*10 Things I Hate About You*): "I had a really great teacher when I was in fourth grade. He taught history, and I hated history. But he was the coolest teacher—he was the one that got me interested in history and reading and stuff. And I know this sounds corny, but he always said we could do whatever we wanted if we followed our dreams."

Adam Sandler (actor): Michael Clemons taught U.S. government at Adam's high school. He admits: "Every day, I used to look forward to the class Adam was in, even though he was a pain. But he was very funny. Just when I was ready to put my hands around his throat and strangle him, he'd look up at me and say, 'You know, Mr. Clemons, you're my favorite teacher.' And I'd start laughing."

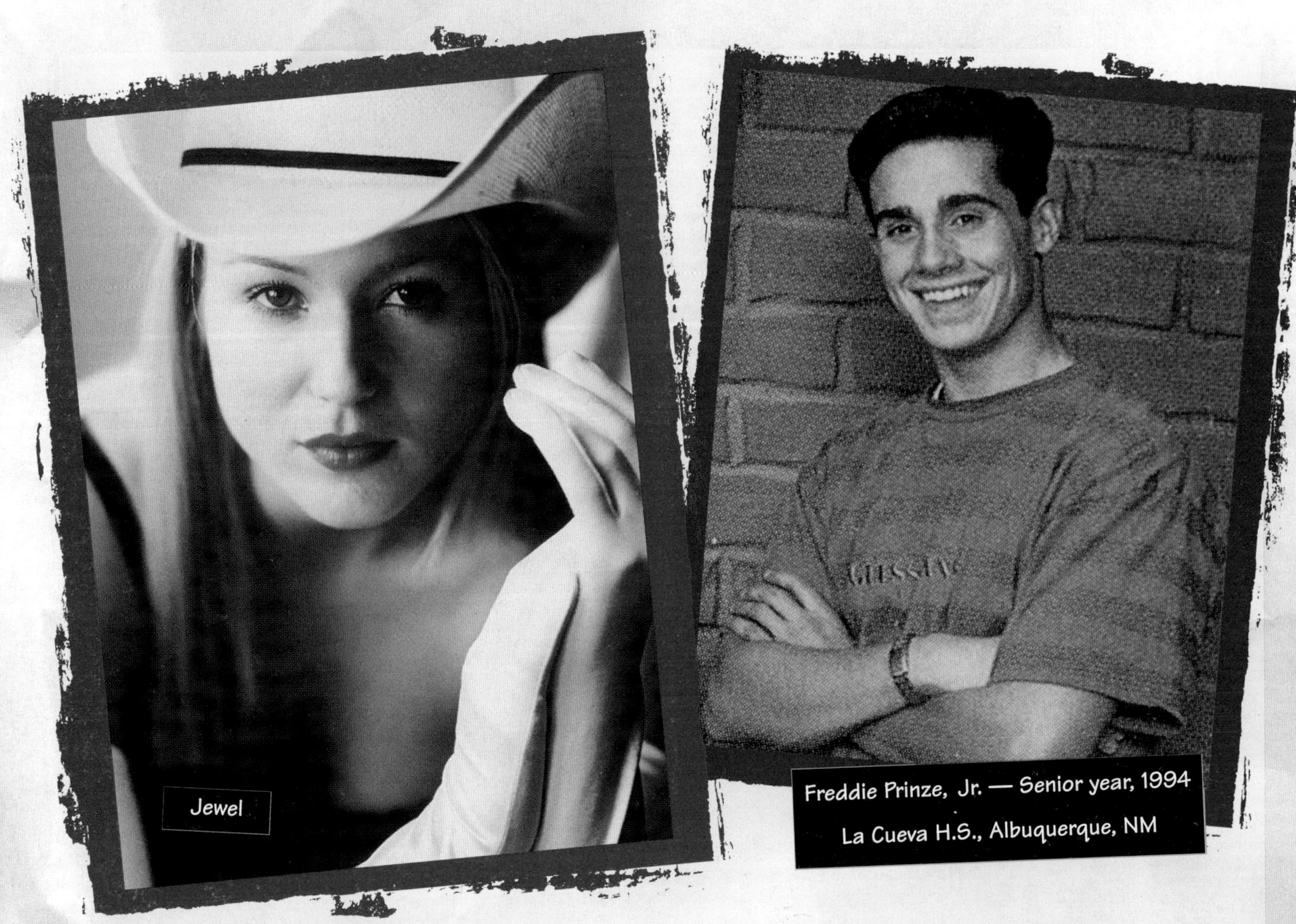
Jewel

Freddie Prinze, Jr. — Senior year, 1994
La Cueva H.S., Albuquerque, NM

Britney Spears (singer): "I had a teacher—her name was Miss Hughes. She was really sweet. She taught me in third grade and I really learned a lot that year. And it wasn't because she was being strict or whatever, she was just an awesome teacher."

Freddie Prinze, Jr. (*She's All That*): Freddie's twelfth-grade literature teacher, Patsy Boeglin, encouraged him to consider drama after he read *Oedipus Rex* in class. "I think everybody could see his passion," Ms. Boeglin recalls.

Brad Fischetti (LFO): "My eighth-grade teacher, Mrs. Nagilia, was my favorite teacher—she trusted in me."

Jewel (singer):Jean Parsons, an instructor at Interlochen Center for the Arts. "The understanding was that [Jewel] could practice her guitar during her breaks," remembers Ms. Parsons.

Devin (LFO): "My high school English teacher, Mr. Charbonneau, was my favorite. He worked us really hard, but he made it fun. He always believed in me."

Michael Rosenbaum (*Zoe, Duncan, Jack, and Jane*): "My favorite teacher was Mrs. Rowe. She taught history class and made it interesting—that's the most important thing a teacher can do."

Scott Foley (*Felicity*): "My favorite teacher was Mr. Heidi and my favorite subject was his class—it was poetry. I didn't write poetry before his class, but because of Mr. Heidi, I did."

David Boreanaz (*Angel*): My favorite teacher was my Spanish teacher—I can't think of her name. I went to an all-boys school and she was gorgeous. All the boys in the class loved her."

Nadia Nascimento (*Animorphs*): "Mr. Burritt—he was my acting teacher all through high school. He taught me the true fundamentals of being an actor. The first thing is you have to find yourself before you find the character. It's a process."

David Boreanaz

Nadia Nascimento

Fave Subjects

* **Monica:** "Algebra II because it made me think."
* **Brandi of Blaque:** "History, English, lunch, and PE."
* **Shamria of Blaque:** "Biology and lunch."
* **Natina of Blaque:** "Biology and lunch—and anything about law."
* **Ryan Phillippe:** "Drama because I didn't find myself that interesting and I wasn't the most outgoing person."
* **Bob Moffatt:** "Social studies, you know, kinda like history, learning about the explorers and things."
* **Clint Moffatt:** "Literature because I find it really easy."
* **Dave Moffatt:** "I like science and Spanish."
* **Seth Green:** "Art—my mom's an artist, so I've got a thing for sketching."
* **Brandy:** "Math. Everything else—science, social studies, history, English—came easier to me but I enjoyed pushing myself to learn math."
* **Brad Fischetti:** "In grade school it was gym class—it was a break from the day. In high school I liked algebra and geometry because I had really good teachers."
* **Rich Cronin:** "I liked history and English."
* **Nick Carter:** "Science, history, English, and gym."
* **Howie Dorough:** "Math!"
* **A.J. McLean:** "English, history."
* **Kevin Richardson:** "History and geometry."
* **J Brown:** "English and physics."
* **Ritchie Neville:** "Drama."
* **Sean Conlon:** "Music, English, and math."
* **Kevin Connelly:** "Social studies."
* **Abs Breen:** "My favorite subject was art—and English. I also liked languages a lot."
* **Devin:** "My favorite subject was science. It was easy—I like science fiction and science class was the closest thing to it."
* **Jessica Biel:** "Biology class is the best! I love anatomy and blood and guts. I like doing science experiments."

Jessica Biel

David Gallagher

Seth Green

* **David Gallagher:** "I love science. Right now we're learning about bacteria and viruses. It's cool to know there are millions and trillions of little things everywhere, but you can't see them."
* **Nicholas Brendon:** "My favorite subject was when the bell rang after sixth period!"
* **Michael Rosenbaum:** "My favorite subject was drama class, because I was able to get out of my body and scream and be somebody else."
* **David Boreanaz:** "Spanish."
* **Joshua Jackson:** "Lunch and recess."
* **Brooke Nevin:** "Math—I'm not a whiz or anything, but I like the whole problem-solving."

Worst Subjects

* **Gavin Rossdale:** "Math and science—I just knew I wouldn't need them, so they kind of went over my head."
* **Mark Wahlberg:** "Science—my teacher was pretty, so I paid more attention to her than to my books!"
* **Rich Cronin:** "I hated math to the point where it made me sick to my stomach."

YUCK!

"In science lab, I dissected a squid—so cool, but soooo stinky! I spent the afternoon letting people smell my hands."—Mackenzie Rosman of *7th Heaven*

Best Memories: Let the Good Times Roll!

Lisa Leslie

Brandy

Remember when you pulled an all-nighter for a science test — and aced it? Or the time you landed the lead in your class play? Or when you were elected a class officer? Join some of your favorite superstars as they recall the good times.

Kevin Richardson of Backstreet Boys: "My favorite memory was when we won our homecoming football game. I played fullback on offense. We were the underdogs."

Lisa Leslie of the WNBA: "In fifth grade I brought my mom and her eighteen-wheel truck to school. My mother was a truck driver. She parked the truck in front of the school, and the kids got to climb inside. They loved it. I became very popular after that."

Shaquille O'Neal of the L.A. Lakers: "When I was in grammar school, I appeared in *Little Red Riding Hood*. I played a tree."

Derek Jeter of the N.Y. Yankees: "I was around eleven and I asked a girl named Sasha out. She said yes. And she was my first kiss — right in the hallway at school."

Shawn Ashmore of *Animorphs*: "After-school snacks! I used to love coming home and having nachos. I would make nachos with salsa and put Tabasco sauce on them. I like spicy foods."

Joshua Jackson of *Dawson's Creek*: "When I go back to Vancouver, I drive straight over to Nat's New York Pizzeria and order a chicken parmesan hero. That's my favorite thing on earth! I first ate there when I was a little kid. Then, when I got to high school, I started going every day. It's a block and a half away from the school, and it's where everybody went for lunch."

Grant Hill of the Detroit Pistons: "My first crush — Ellen Butler. I was in the second grade and we were in the same class. She lived the next block over from me and there was a hoop with a fiberglass backboard at the house right next door to hers. So I would go over there in the hope that she would come outside. In fact, she's responsible for me being a basketball player, because I became pretty good by practicing over there."

Grant Hill

Derek Jeter

Drama Traumas

"Please tell me this isn't happening. I could have died from embarrassment!"... "I was [in] the red zone—I blushed from head to toe!"... "I'll never live it down!" Everyone has those moments—even your favorite costars.

Ben Affleck (actor): "When I was in high school, I was a chump who was always getting beat up by the bigger kids because I was real small. I was 5′1″. Now I'm 6′1″. I grew a foot in a year. I don't get beat up anymore."

Leelee Sobieski (actor): "On my first day of third grade, I wore a dress while everyone else was wearing something trendy, like boxer shorts with a T-shirt. I felt way out of place. But instead of conforming, I made it a point to wear a weird dress every Friday."

Ben Affleck

Leelee Sobieski

Sinead

Natina of Blaque: "In grade school I had a teacher who had allergies; she always said we were trying to kill her because we wore perfume in her class. She told us the next person who came to class wearing perfume was going to be in trouble. So I come in with a big bottle of perfume and I spray it all in the air because the little boy next to me passed gas all the time. It smelled like hard-boiled eggs and licorice. The teacher came up to me and starts screaming, 'You're trying to kill me!' I almost got thrown out of school!"

Joey McIntyre (singer): "I was in parochial school and sat in the front row of my history class. I was looking at something in my book, and I wasn't listening. The teacher didn't like it when I wasn't listening. I kept looking down and after a few minutes, out of nowhere, this eraser hits me on the head. It was all chalked up, so this cloud of chalk comes rising out of my head, and everyone's laughing. It really caught me by surprise because usually I was an attentive student. The teacher looked at me to see how I would react, but I didn't get emotional. Everybody needs a wake-up call, I guess."

Sinead of B*Witched: "The naughtiest thing I did at school was persuading my mum to let me have some eggs and flour to throw over people. I got suspended 'cause I covered everyone in horrible gunk."

Nadia Nascimento of *Animorphs*: "I remember going into seventh grade scared because it was my last year [in elementary school—in Ontario high school is from eighth grade to twelfth grade]. It was because I knew high school was inevitable, and we would be little fish!"

Zachery Ty Bryan of *Home Improvement*: "In third grade, I wore corduroy pants and rolled my left pant leg up over my calf. I thought I was the coolest!"

Jim Carrey (actor): "I remember being sent out of the room a lot. I was like a disease. The teacher told me I was infectious.... On my report card were the words, 'Jim finishes his work first so he can bother the other kids.'"

Ashton Kutcher of *That '70s Show*: "I was a wrestler in high school, and [the team] had this initiation for the freshmen. Everybody gets different things done to them—very nasty things. I got duct-taped to a pole on the basketball court just before the girls' basketball practice. They all came out and had their little giggle and walked away."

Jim Carrey

Adam Frost of *Hang Time*: "When I was in junior high, I [liked] this girl. We were [playing] volleyball in gym, so everybody was in shorts. I was talking to the girl, and one of her girlfriends came up from behind and 'pantsed' me — pulled my shorts right down to my ankles! I blushed and pulled them back. I was paranoid for about two years after that, and I made totally sure, for the rest of my high school years, that my drawstrings were always tied tight. I'll tell you, those things are never going to come down again."

Christopher Ralph
Christina Ricci

A+ (rap star): "When I was about thirteen or fourteen I started getting out of control, cutting class, and then my first single came out and it was making a lot of noise, and I found myself being very distracted. I would go to after-show parties and come home 'round two or four in the morning. . . . I got left back. In the eighth grade, I had to go to summer school and spend the whole summer studying to get back to my original grade."

Christopher Ralph of *Animorphs*: "I was in kindergarten. For no reason at all—I wasn't even sick, this just happened—I threw up on my math book in front of everybody. It blew my mind. I was just sitting there and there it was. Everyone started laughing."

Christina Ricci (actor): "I wasn't into pranks. I was too shy. In my first year of high school, I was so embarrassed most of the time and so red in the face that I looked like a human tomato."

Nicholas Brendon of *Buffy*: "I redefined teenage angst. While Kelly [Nicholas' identical twin brother] went to parties and out on dates, I remained girlfriendless all four years and had acne, braces [Kelly also had braces], and worst of all, a stutter. . . . I called information once, trying to ask for the Foot Locker store in Canoga Park. But I kept saying, 'C-c-c . . .' Kelly grabbed the phone and shouted, 'Canoga Park! Foot Locker!'"

Meredith Monroe of *Dawson's Creek*: "I went to a two-story high school, and I was walking up the stairs and I fell. It was like 'd-d-d-daaa!' down four stairs! My books went flying and I lost my shoe, but I was too mortified to get it. My face was bright red, and this guy walks up to me and goes, 'Is this your shoe?' At lunch, my friends were like, 'Some girl fell down the stairs.' I was like, 'Yeah, I heard about that!'"

Andre Rison of the Kansas City Chiefs: "Remember the fitness test we used to have to take (in school) with the chin-ups, the push-ups? I was doing pull-ups, and I was trying so hard to break the record that my nose started to run! I ran out of the class, out of the gym, and to the bathroom. That was the most embarrassing moment of my life."

Topher Grace of *That '70s Show*: "I went to ask a girl to the Christmas dance. She laughed at me, and then said, 'Oh, you're serious.'"

Lisa Kudrow of *Friends*: "I got my dress on the day of the prom, and it was so awful that I called up my date and canceled."

David Boreanaz of *Buffy* and *Angel*: "I was trying to get into high school and I had to meet with one of the headmasters. My pants ripped right down the seat, and then I had to do the interview. Needless to say, I didn't get in."

Meredith Monroe

Chris O'Donnell

Scott Robinson of FIVE: "Because I'm dyslexic, exams were a nightmare for me at school. I was so [nervous] in one that I scribbled all over the exam sheet and wrote 'I'm a fish,' then signed my name. The exam was meant to be two hours long, and I had an hour longer than everyone else because of my dyslexia, but after ten minutes I said, 'I'm going now,' and got up and left. The teacher was like, 'But you've still got two hours and fifty minutes left,' and I said, 'Look, even if you give me three days, I'm not going to be able to finish it. I don't know any more answers.' It was awful!" (On a happier note, a teacher started working with Scott on a one-to-one basis, and he began to overcome his learning disability.)

Chris O'Donnell (actor): "I was so focused on getting into a good college that I studied four or five hours every night."

Christopher Ralph of *Animorphs*: "In high school, I got detention because I skipped PE class. I had to study for a biology class that I was unprepared for. So I'm in the library and I'm studying for the test, and suddenly the principal's voice comes over the PA system, 'Christopher Ralph, come to the office.' So I come in. . . . They were so disappointed in me. They were like, 'Oh, we can't believe you'd do this!' It's not like they caught me doing something awful. The whole thing was so ridiculous."

Yearbook Predictions & Inscriptions

Class Clown or Computer Geek? Cheerleader Captain or Biology Brainiac? There's always one in every class. Can you match your favorite stars with their yearbook notations? (Answers at the bottom of page 35.)

1) Chris Kirkpatrick 2) Mariah Carey

3) Halle Berry

A) School Paper Editor; Honor Society; Cheerleader Squad; Prom Queen

B) "I was selected 'Most Talented' in my high school yearbook."

C) Spring Sing; Perm Queen; Most Likely to Marry a Father Figure

Halle Berry

Mariah Carey

4) Snoop Doggy Dog

5) Keanu Reeves

6) David Boreanaz

7) Howie Dorough

Keanu Reeves

D) Most Likely to Be in a Pop Group; Shortest — "I was still little in my senior year. I grew like four inches."

E) Glee Club; Advanced Placement Driver's Ed; Most Likely to Beat the Rap

F) Friendliest Student

G) Surf Team; Shakespeare Club Dropout; Least Likely to Complete a Sentence

Lance Bass — Sophomore year, 1995
Clinton H.S., Clinton, MA

8) Adam Sandler

10) Chris Klein

9) Lance Bass

H) Most Likely to Be Famous

I) Secretary of the Student Council; Varsity Football; The Who and U2 Fan

J) "Life is like a bowl of punch: It has a wang to it."

Answer Page

Answers to "Guess Who!" on pages 4 – 5!

Photo A: Leonardo DiCaprio—junior year, John Marshall High School Honor Society

Photo B: Jewel singing

Photo C: Adam Sandler wearing glasses and a Mickey Mouse T-shirt

Photo D: Nick Lachey—in a school play as the Cowardly Lion

Photo E: Katie Holmes—senior year in hat and painted face

Photo F: Jeff Timmons—senior year, with a girl holding him

Photo G: Howie Dorough—sophomore year

Photo H: Keri Russell

Answers to pages 32 – 34!

1) Chris Kirkpatrick: d; 2) Mariah Carey: c; 3) Halle Berry: a; 4) Snoop Doggy Dog: e; 5) Keanu Reeves: g; 6) David Boreanaz: i; 7) Howie Dorough: b; 8) Adam Sandler: j; 9) Lance Bass: f; 10) Chris Klein: h

Pet Peeves

Three hours of homework . . . pop quizzes . . . Wednesday's mystery meat lunch . . . the guy who always tries to sneak a peek at your math tests . . . lockers that never open. The list could go on and on. But don't feel like you're the only who goes crazy over these little irritations. Even some of today's hotties had things to complain about in school!

Ryan Phillippe

Ryan Phillippe (actor): "Kids who pull up at school in a brand-new car and swagger up."

Kirsten Dunst (actor): "We just got a [notice] that says you can't have your hair a certain length. They're taking away the individuality of people, and I think that's wrong."

Howie Dorough (*Backstreet Boys*): "In junior high I was really interested in girls, but I could never keep a relationship because I was already career-oriented. . . . A lot of times, I'd end up having a girlfriend for two or three weeks, if I was lucky."

David Gallagher (*7th Heaven*): "When I come back to school during hiatus from *7th Heaven*, there have been people who go, you know, 'Oooh, we're not worthy.' Some people do it seriously, and some people do it in a really mean way. Those people I can't stomach. I'm not patting myself on the back, but I would never go out of my way to make people feel bad, and I don't go out of my way to insult someone or brag."

Brandy — Freshman year, 1993
Hollywood H.S., Hollywood, CA

Abs Breen (FIVE): "Getting detention was the worst! I didn't get a lot, but the times I did, I dreaded it, because it was like, all my friends were going out to play and I had to stay an extra half hour!"

Freddie Prinze, Jr. (actor): "When I was in school, I read a lot of comic books and pretended I was in them and kids would tease me and call me names."

Brandy (*Moesha*): "When I first moved to Los Angeles, school was awful. I was skinny and I wasn't pretty. Girls pulled my hair and tried to jump me!"

* School Lunch *

* "The chicken . . . it's sooooo greasy!" – Tahj Mowry of Smart Guy

* "Sloppy Joes!" – Curtis Williams, Jr., of Parent 'Hood

* "Once I saw black macaroni and cheese. Luckily, my mom packed me lunch that day!" – David Gallagher of 7th Heaven

* "Mashed potatoes with fluorescent yellow gravy and little pieces of fake turkey in it." – Danielle Deutscher of Hang Time

Party Time!

School dances, football games, pep rallies, parties, and, of course, the prom. See how the stars partied hearty, and had fun, fun, fun.

Melissa Joan Hart (actor): "I wore a spectacular dress from the fifties to my prom. It was all black with an Empire waist and a square neck. It had a velvet top, and then it was all crepe below the waist. I loved it. I still have it. I should wear it again."

Jennifer Love Hewitt (actor): "While I was working on the TV show *The Byrds of Paradise* in Hawaii, an extra from the show sent me a small basket of yellow roses—because I'm from Texas—and a note asking me to go to the prom. It was very romantic—and I got to go to the prom in Hawaii!"

Whitney Houston (singer): "I went to my prom with my best friend. My mother dressed me, and I hated my dress—it was purple and white with ruffles. I took it off the minute we left the prom and put my gear on. Then my friends and I partied till seven A.M."

James Van Der Beek (*Dawson's Creek*): "I went to a homecoming dance with a girl who was trying to break up with me. But she said, 'I still really want to go to homecoming with you.' So I went, thinking I was gonna get her back. It was just terrible. It was her high school, so I barely knew anybody else. And she wound up with some other guy."

Charisma Carpenter, Homecoming Court Senior Year, 1988, Chula Vista H.S., Chula Vista, CA

Katie Holmes (*Dawson's Creek*): "Where I come from, there were a lot of football games. I used to always buy new sweaters and go to the football games on the weekends. Although I liked school a lot, I have to admit I sometimes focused more on dances and football games. . . . But since I went to an all-girls school, dances were just terrible. We'd have to ask the boys out. You felt like a bundle of nerves. 'Who's going to ask this guy to the dance?' 'Well, you took him last time, it's my turn.' Then you'd have to phone, which was worse. 'Hi, what are you working on? Listen, do you want to go to this dance? Okay, 'bye. See you in three weeks.' It made for a horrible evening."

Brandy (*Moesha*): Kobe Bryant was still a senior in high school when he signed with the L.A. Lakers. He met Brandy at the Essence Awards, and asked her right then and there to go to his senior prom with him. "It was a really big deal," recalls Brandy, who hadn't ever gone to a prom. "I didn't think anyone would ever ask. But I couldn't answer right away because I had to check with my mom. So I called him four days later . . . and on May 25th I went to Philadelphia to go to the Lower Merion High School prom with Kobe! It was great!"

Beverley Mitchell (*7th Heaven*): "My best time in school so far was when my friends and I went to see No Doubt. We went backstage, and we got to hang out!"

Don't Look!

"My best guy friends were the crazy people at school, and they would streak across the yard. I would cry laughing."—Tatyana Ali

Boo-hoo!

"I didn't have one date in high school."—Nicholas Brendon

Extracurricular Activities

James Van Der Beek

Charisma Carpenter — Senior year, 1988

Check out how our future stars spent their time when they weren't hitting the books!

James Van Der Beek: Football — until he was injured in junior high, then theater; National Honor Society, student proctor; choir.

Charisma Carpenter: Cheerleading

Andrew Keegan: "My first [acting] job was as a co-host on a Saturday-morning TV special called *Rhythm and Jam*. At that time, I was trying to play basketball in high school, too. My coach complained I was missing practices and I said, 'Look. I'm going to be a movie star.' It was a joke, but I was always confident."

Mase

David Boreanaz — Senior year, 1987
Malvern Prep., Philadelphia, PA

Nicholas Brendon — Senior year, 1989
Chatsworth H.S., Los Angeles, CA

David Boreanaz: Football — he played wide receiver and defensive back.

Mase: Basketball — he even played in the city championship at NYC's Madison Square Garden.

Josh Harnett: Football — until he injured his knee.

Shamari of Blaque: "When I was in eighth grade, I wanted to sing and all I ever wanted was a record deal. So I would go to school and tell people, 'I got a record deal with Sony music and I'm working with Puff Daddy. You wanna be in my group?' I'd be lying just to get them to be in my homemade group. Then I would look in the phone book and find little production companies like 'No Name Records' and call them up and ask them to come and listen to my group!"

Britney Spears: Gymnastics — that's really her doing the flips in her video ". . . Baby One More Time."

Jessica Biel: She was on her school's basketball and soccer teams.

Jewel: In ninth grade, Jewel joined a rap group called La Creme — her group name was "Swiss Miss."

Chris O'Donnell: French club, student council, yearbook staff

Lance Bass

Boris Cabrera

Kevin Richardson, playing Conrad Birdie in "Bye Bye Birdie" — Senior year, 1989 Estill County H.S., Irvine, KY

Julia Stiles (*10 Things I Hate About You*): Modern dance classes, drama club

Justin Timberlake: President of his middle school's Beta Club, student council

Boris Cabrera of *Animorphs*: Wrestling — he was California State High School Champion Wrestler in 1997.

Give Me a B-R-A-N-D-Y!

"In high school I was tutored, so I didn't go to dances, join clubs, and stuff like that. I always wanted to be a cheerleader. At least with *Moesha*, I can have a little glimpse of that." —Brandy

Big Man on Campus!

"In school, I had to do everything. I was president of this, president of that, in this club, in that. Student Council. Honor Society." —Lance Bass

School Directory

Does your school have any famous alumni? Check out the list below and find out—you may even have a famous star's old locker or desk!

Jennifer Aniston: LaGuardia High School of Music and the Arts, New York, NY

Shawn Ashton of *Animorphs*: Turner Fenton High School, Toronto, Ontario

Brandy: Hollywood High School, Hollywood, CA (9th grade); tutored (10th-12th grade)

Neve Campbell: National Ballet School of Canada

Johnny Depp: Miramar High School, Miramar, FL

Cameron Diaz: Long Beach Polytechnic High School, Long Beach, CA

Leonardo Di Caprio: Los Angeles Center for Enriched Studies (up to 10th grade); John Marshall High School (11th grade); tutored (12th grade)

Brendan Fraser: Upper Canada College Preparatory School, Toronto, Ontario

Melissa Joan Hart: Professional Children's School, New York, NY; Dr. Phillips High School, Orlando, FL

Ethan Hawke: Princeton Day School, Princeton, NJ

Jennifer Love Hewitt: Laurel Springs High School, Ojai, CA

Lauryn Hill: Columbia High School, Maplewood, NJ

Monica: Atlanta Country Day School, Atlanta, GA

Nadia Nascimento of *Animorphs*: Argyle High School, Vancouver, Canada

Brooke Nevin of *Animorphs*: Leaside High School, Toronto, Ontario

Chris O'Donnell: Loyola Academy, Wilmette, IL

Freddie Prinze, Jr.: Sandia Prep and La Cueva High School, Albuquerque, NM

Christopher Ralph of *Animorphs*: Prince of Wales Collegiate High School, St. Johns, Newfoundland

Keanu Reeves: Toronto Theater Arts High School, Toronto, Ontario

Christina Ricci: Professional Children's School, New York, NY

Keri Russell: Highland Ranch High School, Highland Ranch, CO

Winona Ryder: Petaluma High School, Petaluma, CA

Alicia Silverstone: San Mateo High School; Beverly Hills High School

Scott Speedman: American Academy of Dramatic Arts, Pasadena, CA

LFO: The Cool Guys

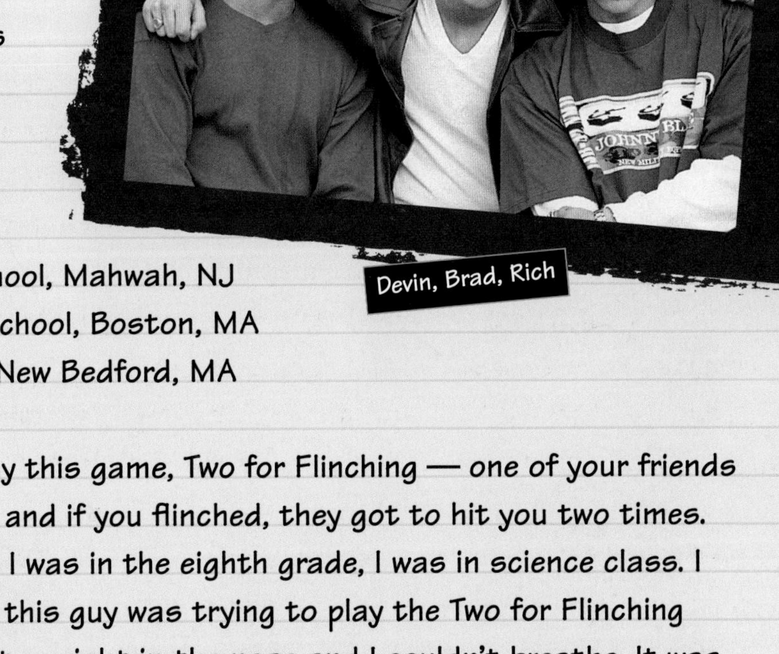

Devin, Brad, Rich

Uh-oh! Sounds like Rich, Brad, and Devin were not teachers' pets . . . maybe teachers' pests! You make the call.

Schools:

Brad Fischetti: Mahwah High School, Mahwah, NJ
Rich Cronin: Sacred Heart High School, Boston, MA
Devin: New Bedford High School, New Bedford, MA

Brad: "In school we used to play this game, Two for Flinching — one of your friends would go like this [a fake punch], and if you flinched, they got to hit you two times. We did it all the time. Once, when I was in the eighth grade, I was in science class. I turned around unexpectedly, and this guy was trying to play the Two for Flinching game. He punched me by accident — right in the nose and I couldn't breathe. It was right after we watched some movie about death in science class, so I thought I was dying. My mom had to come home from work, and I thought she'd be compassionate, but she was like, 'Get over here! Let's go home!' I was like, 'Mom!!!! I just got punched in the nose!'"

Rich: "Once in high school, I got my hands on some stink bombs. I found them in this little hobby shop. I had ten bucks, so I bought them. I go to school, and I'm in the hallway and I put one on the floor and crush it. But it didn't smell, so I thought they were no good and I'd return the rest. I went down the hall to the bathroom, and when I came out there was this awful stench — I almost got sick myself! It was horrible. It smelled like rotten eggs times a million. I got into big trouble because of that stuff!"

Devin: "People from my high school would probably remember the time I forgot the words to the song 'Wild Flower' at the junior banquet. I repeated the same line twice and I just started laughing. I was, like, 'I forgot the words!'"

Will Smith: Class Clown

Think Will is funny and charming now? Newsflash: He was always making his classmates crack up.

School: Our Lady of Lourdes Junior High School; Overbrook Park High School, Philadelphia, PA

School Nickname: "Prince Charming" — the teachers dubbed him this for his ability to always talk his way out of trouble.

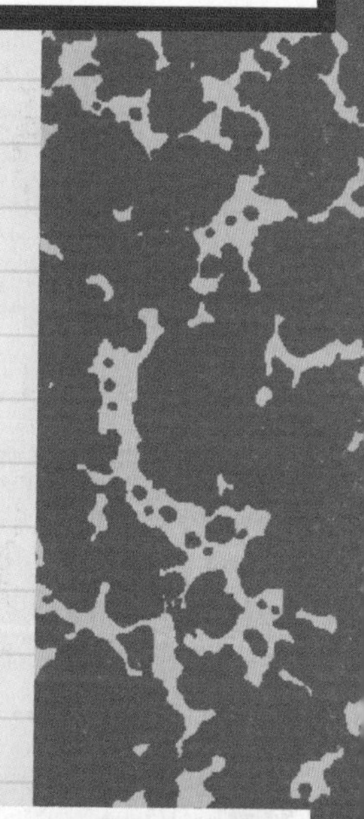

"I always used to get into silly trouble, but I was always so charming, I could smooth talk my way out of any situation. . . . Whenever the teacher was up at the board, I would say something to crack up the entire back of the room. When I saw the teacher start to turn around, my face would go completely blank, like, 'These fractions are so perplexing.' The teacher would go [to some other guy], 'What's so funny, Jimmy?' And the poor guy didn't even start it, but he was holding the bag. Even with that, I got [good] grades — mainly to please my parents. I didn't think I'd ever use what I learned. But in my rap and as an actor, it's amazing how much of what I did learn comes back to me. It all pays off in the end. I just didn't know it then."

Adam Sandler: Laugh Riot

By the age of ten Adam knew he was meant to be a comedian, so he turned his classroom into a comedy club and started to perfect his routine!

School: Manchester Central High School, Manchester, NH

"Until sixth grade, I did really well in school. All of a sudden, I said, 'I can't read and be so serious in class anymore.' I don't know why, but I just started goofing off. I decided to have fun. . . . I was a class clown. I did try to make people laugh when I could, but I'd pick and choose times to be funny — ones that wouldn't get me in trouble."

98° = A+

Before they were heating up the music scene, the 98° guys were steaming up their classrooms!

Schools:

Jeff Timmons: Washington High School, Massillon, OH
Nick Lachey: School for Creative & Performing Arts, Cincinnati, OH
Drew Lachey: School for Creative & Performing Arts, Cincinnati, OH
Justin Jeffre: School for Creative & Performing Arts, Cincinnati, OH

Jeff: "My senior year, I dated a girl who dumped me about two weeks before the prom. So I wound up going with someone who was sort of her rival. I hardly knew her. I kissed my date right in front of my ex-girlfriend, who got so upset. It was the best feeling in the world, because she'd absolutely broken my heart."

Nick: "School is very important to me. You can't do anything without your high school diploma. I wouldn't be here today unless I had school."

Drew: "High school is just a given. You have to get your diploma or your G.E.D., regardless, or you'll be flipping burgers for the rest of your life. I don't even know if they let you flip burgers these days without a high school diploma."

Justin: "Just to have the knowledge of things, like knowing your history, is important. I don't think you can really have an understanding of what is going on in the world today unless you know something about history."

Jewel's School Spirit

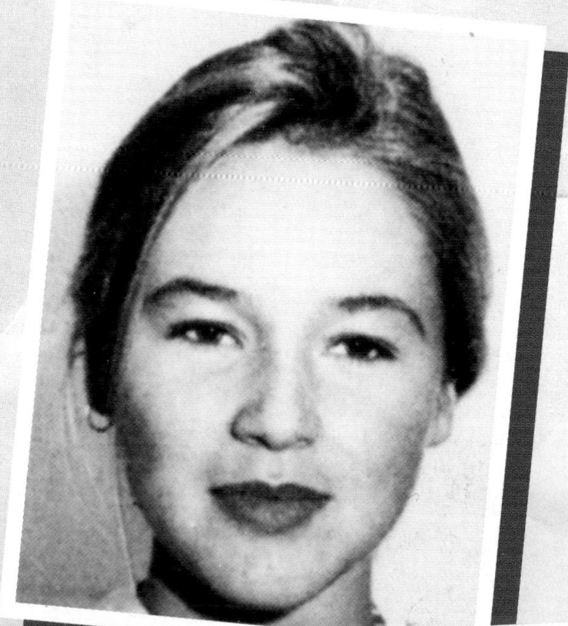

Bonus Factoid!:
In Jewel's yearbook, her name was spelled "Juel."

This singer/songwriter learned very early on that when something doesn't come easily to you at first, you just have to try harder and harder.

School:
Interlochen Fine Arts Academy, Michigan

"I have dyslexia. As a kid, I was always frustrated in class. Initially I loved reading, but then I lost interest. Memorization was really hard because I mixed up the order of letters and numbers, and most of my teachers weren't trained to deal with that. [Then] I took a philosophy course and realized I was very smart and good at thinking. I didn't have to memorize. I could read, think, invent, discuss, and become interactively involved with literature. . . . I have always excelled in writing. I wrote a lot as a kid — stories, essays — and my love of words was really strong."

When she received a Music Scholarship to Michigan's Interlochen Fine Arts Academy for her junior and senior years of high school, Jewel really blossomed. "My two years there were like a turning point," she recalls.

Grant Hill: Reluctant King of the Courts

Grant Hill — Senior year, 1990, South Lakes H.S., Reston, VA

He may be an NBA superstar today, but Grant was never a show-off in school. He knew he had special skills and talents, but he didn't think that made him better than his classmates.

School:
South Lakes High School, Reston, VA

"I hope people don't take this the wrong way, but when I was in school, I wanted nothing more than to be like everyone else. I was fortunate enough to come from a pretty wealthy family; we had nice cars and a big house. But I made my dad drive me to school in a Volkswagen instead of his Mercedes. I didn't want people thinking I was arrogant. I just wanted to be like everyone else."

Grant felt that way even when it came to sports. When Grant was 13 and 6′ 3″, he played on the junior varsity b-ball team. Then the varsity coach asked him to join his team. "I wasn't sure if I wanted to play," Grant says. "So the coach called my dad, and when I got home, my dad was like, 'You're gonna play varsity.' I started crying. I accused him of child abuse. I said, 'You can't make me do something that I don't want to do.' He just said, 'You're gonna play.' From then on I started to really grow to love the sport."

"In high school, I didn't have much of a social life. I got up, went to school, practiced after school, and then came home to do homework. Pretty simple, I guess, but it was a good formula."